Thank you to everyone who contributed to the creation of this tale, especially my wife, Jen; my sister, Dawn; and my mom, Catherine, who all spent countless hours discussing this book. Special thanks to my nephew Zeyn for his invaluable editing and ideas.

© 2025 Timothy M. Porter

All Rights Reserved

ISBN – 979-8-218-60154-6

INTRODUCTION

By Dawn Waheed

*"You're only given one little spark of madness.
You mustn't lose it." - Robin Williams*

My brother, Timmy, has a laugh just like our dad's: it's full, deep, joyful, and reserved only for the truly funny. The unraveling of my father's brain from Lewy Body Dementia is decidedly not funny, but sometimes all we can do is laugh. In this memoir, Timmy will make you laugh out loud at the absurdity of our dad's hallucinations and delusions. But he will also show you how devastating LBD is by giving you a glimpse of the man our father once was.

When we were younger our parents had several Alaskan Malamute dogs, which we took regularly to dog shows. Once, my dad decided they should also learn to pull a sled. When we moved to San Diego, we had a slight problem: we didn't have any snow. This did not deter my father. We bought a sled with wheels and the dogs were trained to pull it with my dad at the helm. During the holiday season one year, my father put on a Santa hat while the rest of us dressed as elves and the dogs pulled us through an outdoor mall like Santa's reindeer. This is one of the best memories I have of my father. I love his willingness to do something silly just for the fun of it.

We can still see the fun side peeking through occasionally, but far too often the disease takes over. Our dad's battle with LBD has affected Timmy more than anyone else. Timmy has been tasked with overseeing my father's finances. He has also been the person our dad goes to most often to help him make sense of the hallucinations, delusions, anxiety, and fears that have become his world.

It has not been easy dealing with our father's illness, especially because we are spread out across the country. Timmy has accepted his role as President and CEO of "The Company" (see the chapter titled "The Family Corporation" to learn more about that) and has done the best he can in very difficult circumstances. If you have a parent or loved one with dementia, you know what it is like to watch them slowly lose their minds. This short memoir, written by my brother about our father, is full of humor, nostalgia, tragedy, and love.

AN UPRISING OF THE MIND

Tim Porter sat by the window of his modest West Virginia apartment. The soft hum of crickets outside barely masking the chaos brewing in his mind. His wife, Ashley, paced quietly around the room, every motion deliberate. Tim had always admired her composure, a trait she had carried from her upbringing in the rural town of Shangrao, China. Her presence was the only thing grounding Tim now as the weight of false accusations and the looming threat of capture bore down on him.

Born in Louisiana in the 1940s, Tim had seen his fair share of upheaval, from the civil rights struggle of the Deep South to the Vietnam War. But nothing had prepared him for the current political unrest gripping his adopted town in West Virginia. The country was a tinderbox, and this town had become the flashpoint. As a guard for the local judiciary, Tim had been tasked with protecting judges prosecuting those fueling the uprising. It was dangerous, thankless work, but he had never been one to shy away from duty.

Then came the fire at the orphanage.

The memory was a raw, festering wound. The orphanage had been a sanctuary, a place where Tim and Ashley volunteered their evenings to help children who had no one else. But that night, flames had engulfed the building, and the inferno claimed the lives of several infants before firefighters could extinguish it. The image of those tiny cribs reduced to ash haunted Tim's every waking moment.

Worse still, Tim had been accused of starting the fire. The evidence was damning—a canister of kerosene with his fingerprints on it; eyewitnesses who swore they saw him near the building just before the flames erupted. But Tim knew the truth: he had been framed. The real culprit was someone tied to the uprising, someone who wanted him off guard duty to weaken the judges' security. Tim even had his name: Roy Beckett. But proving it was another matter.

Now, he and Ashley were fugitives in their own home, the blinds drawn tight and the door bolted shut. Tim picked up the phone, his fingers trembling as he dialed a number he hadn't called in months.

"Dad?" came the voice on the other end.

"Timmy, I need your help," Tim said, his voice hoarse. He hadn't spoken to his son in years, not since a bitter argument had driven them apart. Timmy had pursued a career in technology, a passion he and Tim had once shared. Now, Tim hoped his son's resourcefulness and connections could save his life.

"What's going on?" Timmy asked.

"They're coming for me," Tim said. "I've been framed for the orphanage fire. I need a defense attorney, someone who can untangle this mess."

There was a long pause on the line. Tim could hear the faint sound of a television in the background: it was the nightly news blaring reports of the unrest.

"You're serious?" Timmy finally said.

"Dead serious. They'll arrest me any day now if I don't act fast. And if they do, they'll make sure I never see a courtroom."

Ashley placed a gentle hand on Tim's shoulder, her dark eyes meeting his with quiet reassurance. She had always been his anchor. Her steadfast belief in his innocence gave him strength.

"I'll make some calls," Timmy said, his tone softening. "But you need to lay low. They're probably watching every move you make."

"We know," Tim replied. "That's why I'm calling you. You're the only one I trust."

After hanging up, Tim leaned back in his chair, his hands gripping the armrests as if holding on for dear life. Outside, the distant sound of sirens cut through the night, a grim reminder of how close the danger was.

"Do you think he'll help?" Ashley asked, her voice barely above a whisper.

Tim nodded, though doubt gnawed at him. "He'll come through. He has to."

But as the minutes stretched into hours, Tim couldn't shake the feeling that time was running out. Somewhere out there, Roy Beckett was walking free, while Tim's world burned around him. And unless his son could deliver a miracle, the flames of injustice would consume them all.

My dad called me at least five times a day. He was convinced that he was living through an uprising, trapped in his West Virginia apartment. But it was a delusion. He was safe in Shangrao, living comfortably with his wife.

Confusing dreams with reality often stems from the vividness of the dreams, particularly those that are emotionally charged or closely resemble real-life situations. It is especially common in individuals with conditions that affect cognitive functioning, such as Lewy Body Dementia (LBD).

Lewy Body Dementia is a progressive neurodegenerative disorder that causes a decline in cognitive abilities, affecting memory, attention, and perception. One of its hallmark symptoms is the presence of visual hallucinations. These hallucinations can cause significant distress and confusion.

In addition, LBD often disrupts sleep patterns, leading to more intense and frequent dreams or nightmares. This can further blur the lines between dreams and reality. As a result, those with Lewy Body Dementia may experience heightened anxiety, fear, or confusion due to the persistent uncertainty of their perceptions.

This overlap between dreams and reality is not limited to LBD, but the cognitive and perceptual issues associated with LBD make it particularly challenging for affected individuals. Therefore, it is important to provide appropriate care and support for people with Lewy Body Dementia, especially when managing the emotional and cognitive symptoms.

WHO WAS TIM PORTER?

Tim Porter's story begins in the vibrant streets of New Orleans, a city steeped in history, culture, and community. The eldest of six children, Tim had a childhood as lively as the city itself. With three brothers (Richard, David, and Michael) and two sisters (Mary and Kathy), Tim's home was full of laughter, faith, and a healthy dose of mischief. The Porter family's roots ran deep in the area: their large Catholic family was part of a broader network of relatives that would gather for reunions of up to a thousand people. The stories, shared meals, and profound sense of belonging at these gatherings influenced Tim's identity for the rest of his life.

Tim's upbringing reflected the strong Catholic traditions of the time. He attended Jesuit High School, a prestigious institution that shaped his academic and personal foundation. A proud Blue Jay, he often recounted stories of his time there, painting vivid pictures of what it was like to attend a Catholic high school in the 1960s. From strict nuns to academic challenges to the camaraderie of his classmates, the anecdotes always carried a mix of humor and nostalgia. The discipline and values he learned during those years became a cornerstone of his character.

One tale that stood out involved a summer job cutting down trees. Living next door to a convent added a unique twist to this adventure. One day, the nuns enlisted Tim's help to remove a tree struck by lightning. Ever resourceful, Tim roped his brother Michael into the task. The plan was simple—tie one end of a rope to the tree and the other to Michael to guide its fall. Predictably, nature had its own plan. The tree fell straight into the convent, dragging Michael across the yard in the process. It was a classic Porter escapade, a blend of ingenuity and chaos, and it became part of the family's lore.

After high school, Tim earned a scholarship to Catholic University in Washington, DC, but after one year, he transferred to Louisiana State University at New Orleans (today the University of New Orleans). Thanks to his insatiable curiosity and determination, he graduated with a bachelor's degree in mathematics, setting him on a path to a remarkable career. As the Vietnam War loomed, Tim chose to serve in the Navy, attending Officer Candidate School (OCS). His naval career began aboard the diesel submarine USS Bugara, stationed in San Diego. There, he met his first wife, Catherine.

Tim's Navy tenure was impactful. He served on the USS Blueback in Navy Intelligence and as a navigator on the USS Shreveport. His final post was as a Foreign Officer Course Coordinator in Dam Neck, Virginia, a role that involved hosting international officers and fostering diplomatic relationships. During this time, he also pursued a master's degree in Information Systems at George

Washington University. Balancing his professional and academic responsibilities showcased his commitment to growth and excellence.

After leaving the Navy, Tim transitioned to the private sector, starting at a small software company and relocating the family to San Diego. He later joined SAIC, where he became known for his expertise in managing large Department of Defense contracts. His organized and dependable leadership earned him a strong reputation at the company. In 1993, the family moved to Northern Virginia, where Tim continued his successful tenure with SAIC until retiring in his late 50s. Those years were marked by both professional success and the joys of raising a family, with weekends often spent exploring new places or sharing meals around the dinner table.

Retirement marked the beginning of a new chapter in Tim's life. He immersed himself in learning Mandarin, achieving fluency within a few years. Catherine, who worked at Johns Hopkins University's School for Advanced International Studies, helped him join an immersion program in China. This sparked a six-year period of travel between the U.S. and China, during which Tim embraced new cultures and experiences. While in China, he worked as a professor, consulted for large software companies, and contributed to orphanage projects. His efforts reflected his deep sense of responsibility and his desire to make a difference wherever he went.

But his life took an unexpected turn. He and Catherine divorced. Tim later married Ashley. Tim and Ashley adopted Claire, then known as Dora or Ting, from China. The new family settled back in Northern Virginia, where Tim became a professor at George Mason University. Teaching allowed him to share his wealth of knowledge and passion for learning with a new generation of students.

Tim and his new family built a life in Northern Virginia for nearly two decades while his other children—Jason, Trish, Dawn, and Timmy—lived in different parts of the country. Tim grew ever more distant from his older children. Yet, his life's journey was one of resilience, intellect, and an enduring sense of adventure. His story is a testament to the power of adaptability and purpose, a legacy that continues to inspire those who knew and loved him.

SPINNAKER SHENANIGANS AT THE SCREWPILE REGATTA

In my early twenties, I spent an inordinate amount of time on my dad's Catalina 320, cruising and racing on the Chesapeake Bay. Dad, in his fifties, had become quite the sailing enthusiast: the boat was his pride and joy. Between Wednesday night sails and weekend regattas, we practically lived on the water. One of our favorite events—and the most infamous—was the Screwpile Regatta in Solomons Island, Maryland.

Screwpile was the regatta of regattas on the Chesapeake. Hundreds of boats participated, grouped into divisions based on handicaps or one-designs, and the event's reputation for epic parties had sailors from up and down the East Coast flocking to join. For most participants, the event started with an overnight race from Annapolis to Solomons Island. For us, it started with Dad's latest bold decision: racing with a spinnaker for the very first time.

A spinnaker is a massive, colorful sail designed for downwind sailing. It's also a bit of a beast, requiring skill, timing, and a coordinated crew. But Dad, ever the optimist, declared, "How hard can it be?"—in hindsight that was less a question and more a prediction of impending chaos.

Gathering the Crew

For this maiden spinnaker voyage, I assembled a crew consisting of my sister-in-law Kelly, her husband Growson, and family friend Vince. All three had sailed on my smaller boat before and were familiar with the basic spinnaker maneuvers, which gave us a false sense of competence. We figured, "How different could it be on the Catalina?" Spoiler alert: very different.

We decided to save our first attempt with the spinnaker for the actual race. Because, of course, nothing tests your mettle like trying something completely new in front of hundreds of experienced sailors.

The Great Spinnaker Experiment

On Sunday, for the first race, the sail went up without a hitch. For a brief, glorious moment, we looked like we knew what we were doing. The wind caught the spinnaker, and the boat surged forward. We were flying. Even the veteran sailors in nearby boats gave us approving nods.

We're actually doing this, I thought, equal parts exhilarated and terrified. The spinnaker billowed in the breeze, a riot of color against the sky, and for a fleeting moment, we were the envy of the fleet.

By some miracle, we were in first place. The finish line loomed ahead, and we crossed it triumphantly—to cheers from Dad and stunned silence from the rest of the crew. We had won the race!

The Problem with Winning

But as we crossed the finish line, the wind picked up. The spinnaker, now fully loaded, was pulling us along at an alarming speed. None of us had considered how we were going to get it down.

"Okay, team," Dad said, trying to sound calm. "Let's douse the spinnaker."

We scrambled to the foredeck like a group of clumsy circus performers, grabbing at ropes and fabric. The spinnaker billowed defiantly, refusing to be tamed. We sailed a good half-mile past the finish line, leaving a trail of bemused onlookers in our wake.

Finally, Dad took charge. He let the sail fly free, spilling the wind and allowing us to wrestle it to the deck. The whole operation took ten minutes. We were no longer a sleek, victorious racer but a floundering spectacle. By the end, we were drenched in sweat and laughing at our own ineptitude.

"Well," Dad said, once the sail was safely stuffed below. "We'll call that a learning experience."

Screwpile Proper

The Screwpile Regatta was three days of intense racing and equally intense socializing. By the end of the event, we had solidified our reputation as the team that could somehow win a race despite having no idea what we were doing. The parties were as legendary as advertised, with tales of our spinnaker debacle spreading faster than the free Dark and Stormys.

We spent each evening recounting the day's races with other sailors, swapping exaggerated tales of victory and near disaster. Dad became a minor celebrity, his penchant for storytelling growing with each retelling of our spinnaker escapade. By the end of the regatta, we had gained a few friends and a few nicknames.

The Cruise Home

As we packed up the boat to head home, Dad looked out over the Chesapeake, grinning like a man who had just conquered Everest. The cruise back to the Rhode River was a serene contrast to the whirlwind of the regatta. The water was calm, and the late afternoon sun cast golden hues across the bay. We took our time, recounting the weekend's chaos and triumphs while munching on sandwiches and sipping lukewarm coffee.

Dad, ever the storyteller, embellished our spinnaker victory with each retelling, much to the crew's amusement. "Did you see their faces when we crossed the line?" he asked for the third time, gesturing dramatically. "Priceless!" We laughed, humoring him, as the rhythmic sound of water lapping against the hull set a peaceful backdrop.

Halfway home, the sun dipped below the horizon, painting the sky in shades of orange and purple. The calm waters reflected the fading light, creating a moment of quiet beauty that made all the chaos worth it. By the time we reached the familiar shores of the Rhode River, we were tired but happy, already looking forward to the next adventure.

"Next time," Dad said, leaning back in his seat, "we'll practice beforehand."

We never did. But the stories, the laughter, and those chaotic moments on the water made those years unforgettable.

PHONE CALLS IN THE NIGHT

It all started with the phone calls.

Remember when you were a kid, and your dad was the guy who always seemed to know everything? He was a walking encyclopedia with a sense of humor that bordered on dad-level cringe, but it was our dad-level cringe, so we tolerated it. But fast-forward a few decades, and all that's left is a shadow of that man—someone who can't remember if he's on the phone with his son or a pizza delivery guy.

Jason, the oldest, was the first to notice something strange. "Dad just called me and asked how Timmy was doing," he said, scratching his head. "I told him, 'He's fine, Dad.' Then Dad asked me again two minutes later. And again, an hour later."

At first, my siblings and I thought it was just old age creeping up on him. After all, he had been around for a while. But when Dad started calling at three in the morning asking if we wanted to join him for breakfast (and then called again an hour later, wondering why we hadn't shown up yet), we knew something was off. We'd answer, listen to him repeat the same questions, hear his confused ramblings, and just think, huh, that's odd. Maybe he just needs more fiber.

It was like we were playing a game of telephone where the signal kept getting worse. The calls started coming at all hours. I remember receiving a call from Dad at 11 PM one night.

"Hey, you got any plans for Christmas?" he asked.

"Dad, it's March."

"Right, right. Christmas. Forgot. Are you coming?"

"I don't know, we'll see."

"Great! What time does Santa get there?"

I had no idea how to respond. "I think Santa has a different schedule now, Dad."

It was like this for many weeks. Sometimes the phone would ring, and we knew it was Dad without looking. But it was impossible to know what version of Dad we were going to get. Was it the Dad who was still a professor, wise and authoritative, or the one who thought he needed a nap in the middle of a conversation about eggplant fried rice?

The four older siblings had grown distant from our dad, but as the calls continued, we pieced things together. Dad's wife, Ashley, having lost her patience and not understanding what was going on, had moved back to Shangrao six months earlier. Claire, their adopted daughter, was away at college. Our dad was left alone—it seemed like a recipe for disaster. And it was. We learned that he had been losing track of time, mixing up appointments, and, apparently, driving his car down the wrong side of the street. One of his old friends, who had known him for many years, called us with a warning: "You've got to stop him from driving. He can't even remember how to use the turn signal and he ran into a mailbox!"

That's when we all started to talk—well, more like text each other in rapid succession like we were the world's worst secret society.

Jason: "Dad keeps calling me asking if I remember when he gave me that fishing rod. I'm pretty sure he never gave me a fishing rod."

Dawn: "Oh my god, he's been doing the same thing to me. Repeated the same story about his Navy days like ten times last night."

Me: "Weird. He's called me twice today to ask how to use his email."

Then came the bombshell: he wasn't even working anymore. We found out through the grapevine that the university had decided not to renew his contract. His story was that he was "retiring," but considering it wasn't exactly on his terms, to my dad it felt more like being pushed off a metaphorical cliff.

Meanwhile, Dad kept acting like he had nothing to worry about. He called me one day, casually mentioning that he'd been diagnosed with Parkinson's Disease. But he was so matter-of-fact that I barely registered it. "It's no big deal," he said, "just a little shaking in the hands, but it's fine. I'm just a little tired sometimes."

And that was that. No big dramatic speech, just an offhand comment. Parkinson's. No big deal. Like it was just a mild case of the sniffles. We didn't know whether to panic or laugh at his attempt to downplay it. But then, just a few weeks later, Claire came back home for winter/spring/summer break and dropped a bombshell of her own.

"I don't know what's going on, but he's different. I mean, really different. Last semester, he couldn't even figure out how to put the students' grades into the computer. I had to help him do it because he was so confused. And I swear he's talking about things that didn't happen."

His mind was unraveling faster than we could keep up. It wasn't just Parkinson's anymore. Eventually, during a routine doctor's visit, we got our answer. At the tail end of the visit, Dad casually mentioned that he had been experiencing hallucinations.

The doctor almost fell out of his chair. He'd seen Dad several times before but had never heard anything about hallucinations. He referred Dad to a neurologist, who suggested that Lewy Body Dementia might be the cause. The neurologist explained that it was a form of progressive dementia with symptoms overlapping Parkinson's but with the added challenge of cognitive decline and vivid hallucinations. The revelation hit us like a tidal wave.

Now, the doctor didn't outright say it was a definitive diagnosis—because there's no real test for LBD until after you're dead—but based on Dad's symptoms, that was the best guess. Lewy Body Dementia was the *likely* culprit, and let me tell you, the *likely* part didn't make us feel any better.

We started researching. Dawn became the family expert on LBD, sending out group texts full of medical jargon and long-winded explanations about protein deposits in the brain. She started talking to support groups. Jason became Dad's unofficial caregiver, managing his medications and making sure he didn't try to microwave his wallet again. We all had our roles to play, but it felt like we were fumbling in the dark, trying to make sense of a disease that refused to be pinned down.

So there we were. Dad, a man who once commanded lecture halls full of students, who had made his career on his sharp mind, was now struggling to recognize his own family. No more driving, no more teaching, and certainly no more impromptu Christmas calls in March. We were a family trying to rediscover a connection with a father who needed us now more than ever.

So that's how we found out: through a string of strange phone calls, hushed family conversations, and a few awkward doctor appointments. It took us a while to put it all together, but when we finally did, we were left standing in the wreckage of the father we once knew, trying to figure out how we could help him when he couldn't even help himself anymore. It was the start of a journey we never expected but one we knew we had to face together.

Distinguishing normal aging memory problems from Lewy Body Dementia (LBD) is based on the severity and scope of symptoms. With normal aging, occasional forgetfulness, such as misplacing items or struggling to recall a name, is common. But these lapses typically don't interfere significantly with daily life. In contrast, LBD often involves more pronounced cognitive challenges, such as frequent confusion, difficulty with problem-solving, and noticeable memory loss that disrupts daily functioning. Additionally, LBD is marked by unique symptoms such as visual hallucinations, movement difficulties resembling Parkinson's disease, and rapid fluctuations in alertness or cognitive ability.

THE WORKERS: A MOST UNHELPFUL BUNCH

Living alone wasn't easy for Dad, even before Lewy Body Dementia decided to throw a full-on carnival. But once the hallucinations kicked in, things went from "quiet evenings alone" to "The Twilight Zone meets HGTV." His house became the stage for a parade of humanoid hallucinations he called "the workers."

Now, these weren't your average hallucinations. Oh no. The workers had flair. Imagine if a table and a chair got together to choreograph a Broadway show and recruited a gang of blankets and pillows to play the lead roles. Their legs were the spindly, polished wood of dining room furniture, and their torsos were a chaotic tangle of fabric. They didn't just stand around—they were a lively, bustling crew. Whether they were "cleaning," "fixing things," or engaging in an impromptu dance party, these guys were the life of the house.

Dad, however, was not impressed. "You'd think after four hours of cleaning, the place would at least look halfway decent," he'd grumble. But no. Every morning, he'd wake up to the same chaos he'd left behind. Crumbs still on the counter, the mail scattered across the dining room table, and the dishes in the sink very much unwashed. "It's like they're unionized against actual productivity," he'd say with a huff.

One night, Dad tried to take a stand. The workers were at it again, clattering around the house, dragging imaginary brooms across the floor and rearranging furniture that didn't need rearranging. The racket was unbearable. "Would you guys keep it down? Some of us are trying to sleep here!" he shouted. Of course, this only seemed to encourage them. The dancing got more frenetic, and someone—possibly a blanket with a Napoleon complex—started drumming on the coffee table.

Ignoring them didn't always work either. "It's hard to ignore a chair-leg man pirouetting across the living room," he'd admit. "Especially when he's singing."

But the workers weren't all bad. There was one night when they set up an elaborate conga line that marched through the kitchen, out the back door, and around the yard. Dad admitted he'd almost joined in just to see what would happen, but he figured the neighbors might have questions. Still, the image of blanket torsos and chair-leg dancers wiggling their way through the yard stuck with him—and with us, whenever he retold the story.

Still, the workers could be downright exhausting. Their nocturnal antics often left Dad more tired in the morning than when he went to bed. He took to muttering under his breath as he shuffled into the kitchen for his coffee. "I don't know why I even bother. They're just going to 'help' again tonight."

The most baffling part for Dad was how realistic they seemed. He'd watch them sweep imaginary dust piles or fold nonexistent laundry with such conviction that he'd start to question his own reality. Were the workers really a hallucination? Or was he just really bad at noticing clean-up progress? It was a philosophical puzzle for the ages.

In the end, the workers became an odd sort of company. Annoying, yes, but also entertaining in their own bizarre way. Dad would tell their stories with a mix of exasperation and fondness, as if the workers were relatives who overstayed their welcome during the holidays. "If they ever figure out how to make themselves useful," he'd say, "I'll be the first to put them on the payroll. But until then, they're just furniture with delusions of grandeur."

The house went without much cleaning, though it wasn't for lack of effort on the part of the imaginary workforce. Their nightly antics may have involved endless sweeping, folding, and rearranging, but their results were spectacularly underwhelming, leaving the real mess untouched and adding an extra layer of surreal disorder. Sometimes, they seemed to compete with each other, racing to "clean" the same imaginary mess, leaving trails of imaginary dust clouds behind them like cartoon characters.

The workers showed up in unexpected places. While staying at my house in North Carolina, Dad stood in the sauna room, squinting suspiciously toward the guest room where he was staying. Lucas, our youngest son, was heading to the shower when Dad stopped him. "What are those ladies doing in there?" Dad asked, his tone a mix of confusion and irritation.

Lucas froze in surprise. Worried, he cautiously stepped into the guest room to investigate and reassured Dad that there was no one there. Dad reluctantly accepted that it must have been "the workers" at it again. The encounter left Lucas scratching his head and Dad grumbling about the never-ending antics of his uninvited, unhelpful 'crew.'

The workers even managed to make road trips feel like an episode of a bizarre reality show. On one drive from Virginia to North Carolina, Dad's attention was rapidly darting between the car's interior and the other vehicles zooming by. Keeping a watchful eye on Dad, I couldn't quite figure out what was going on. Then, out of nowhere, Dad leaned forward and started trying to roll down the window.

"What are you doing, Dad?" I asked, glancing nervously at the road.

"Roll the window down!" Dad insisted.

"Why?" I pressed, unsure whether to humor him.

"Debbie keeps jumping from the dash to the trucks next to us. She scurries along the side of the truck and then jumps back in."

"Well, if she's managing to do all that with the window up, we're probably fine to leave it closed," I suggested.

Dad, apparently satisfied with this logic, sat back in his seat and resumed his watchful vigil of Debbie's antics. Meanwhile, I couldn't decide whether to laugh or pull over to process the absurdity of the moment.

Life with Lewy Body Dementia was anything but ordinary, but if there was one thing Dad proved, it was that a good sense of humor could make even the most surreal situations a little more bearable. LBD hallucinations are often described as vivid and hyper-real, and can range from benign and whimsical to deeply unsettling. They can lead to moments of confusion and frustration. But maybe, just maybe, the workers weren't there to drive Dad crazy—perhaps they were just there to keep him company, even if they were the messiest houseguests he'd ever had.

Dealing with hallucinations in Lewy Body Dementia requires a careful and compassionate approach. Doctors typically advise caregivers to remain calm and avoid challenging the person's perception of reality, as this can escalate anxiety or distress. Instead, they recommend acknowledging the patient's feelings and gently redirecting their attention to something more reassuring or familiar. Creating a safe, well-lit, and quiet environment can help reduce the likelihood of hallucinations. It's essential to monitor for triggers, such as overstimulation, stress, or changes in routine, and minimize these whenever possible. Medications may be considered in severe cases, but doctors usually prioritize non-pharmacological interventions first due to the sensitivity of Lewy Body Dementia patients to antipsychotic drugs, which can worsen symptoms. Regular communication with healthcare professionals is vital to tailor strategies to the individual's needs and ensure the patient's safety and comfort.

SELLING THE HOUSE

Convincing Dad to sell his house was a bit like trying to persuade a squirrel to hand over its nuts. For dad the house represented years of memories, mismatched furniture, and a junk drawer so robust it could survive an apocalypse. But the doctor had made it clear: Dad couldn't live alone. Jason's home was a stopgap—it wasn't built for long-term elder care. And none of us siblings was in a position to take Dad in indefinitely. We had no choice but to sell the house and find Dad an assisted living arrangement.

The problem? Dad was not on board.

"I'm not ready for a home," he declared with the conviction of someone who believed nursing homes were portals to another dimension.

"It's not a 'home,' Dad. It's assisted living," Jason explained for the millionth time.

"You can call it what you want. I'm not going," Dad replied, crossing his arms in defiance.

This resistance was from a man who tried to microwave coffee in the toaster. Meanwhile, Ashley had made it abundantly clear from her perch in China that she was not coming back to the States. Ever.

The first hurdle was emotional. Dad's house wasn't just a building: it was a mausoleum of memories and oddities. The second hurdle was practical: the house was, to put it politely, a disaster. Years of deferred maintenance had taken their toll. The yard looked like a nature preserve. The garage was a maze of half-empty paint cans, rusty tools, and something unidentifiable we collectively agreed not to touch.

Jason, living closest to Dad in Northern Virginia, became the project manager for this Herculean task.

"We'll just take it one step at a time," he said during the first family call. He sounded hopeful, though we all knew he was deeply regretting volunteering for this role.

Trish flew in from Mississippi, Dawn from Arizona, and I drove up from North Carolina. Claire, juggling her junior year at Virginia Tech, managed what she could on weekends. We each took shifts at Dad's house, sorting, packing, and trying not to cry—or laugh. Often, it was both.

The Packing Chronicles

Dad and I discovered a dusty box while sorting through the chaos, uncovering a treasure trove of items from Dad's father, Joseph Porter. Grandpa Joe was a remarkable man who served in the Army during World War II, carrying a sense of duty and devotion that shaped not only his life but also the expectations he passed down to his family. A devout Catholic, Joe attended mass daily in his later years. He lived a life rooted in faith and discipline. The box held a deeply personal collection: Grandpa's worn leather wallet with cherished photos of Grandma, his weathered bible with notes tucked between the pages, the small amount of cash he had on hand when he passed, and a few mementos from his Army days, including a medal and an old service patch. It was a poignant reminder of the legacy Dad was striving to uphold, even amid his current struggles.

"Why do you have seventeen flashlights?" Trish asked one afternoon.

"You never know when you'll need light," Dad replied as if this were the most reasonable answer in the world.

"And the fifteen-year-old cans of tuna?" Dawn quipped, holding up a can that looked more like a museum relic than a pantry staple.

"They don't go bad," Dad insisted.

The sorting process was like uncovering archaeological layers of Dad's life. There were stacks of National Geographics, receipts from the 1980s, and an entire collection of pots and pans underneath the master bathroom sink.

We also had to deal with Dad and Claire's dogs. The older one was rehomed with Claire—because nothing says college life like juggling midterms and a geriatric

Goldendoodle—and the younger one was already with her. This was a small victory in a sea of logistical nightmares.

Teamwork Makes the Dream Work?

Hiring movers, renting storage units, coordinating contractors—it felt like planning a wedding. Only instead of joy and cake, there was drywall repair and bathroom remodeling. Every task brought a unique flavor of chaos.

"The inspector said the bathroom shower needs replacing," Jason announced during one call.

"Of course it does," I sighed.

"And the roof might have some… issues," Jason continued.

"Define 'issues,'" Trish said, bracing herself.

"It leaks."

"So basically, it's not a roof," Dawn deadpanned.

Dad, oblivious to the mounting expenses, spent most of his energy obsessing over moving back to China to reunite with Ashley, despite her clear uninterest in the idea.

"She'll come around," Dad insisted.

"Sure, Dad," Jason replied, running out of patience but trying to keep things civil.

A Family Affair

Despite the challenges, there were moments of hilarity and bonding. One day, Trish discovered a box labeled "Important Papers" that contained nothing but old menus and expired coupons. Jen, my wife, spent multiple days opening and sorting through piles of mail, uncovering everything from overdue bills to junk mail. And we all had to stifle laughter when Dad tried to supervise the movers and ended up giving them directions to the wrong storage unit.

Eventually, after months of effort and a small fortune in contractor fees, the house was ready to sell. We virtually stood in the empty living room on the final day, exhausted but relieved.

"It's weird," Claire said. "It's like we're saying goodbye to more than just the house."

She wasn't wrong. The house had been a symbol of Dad's independence, however chaotic it may have been. Now, it was a reminder of how much things had changed for all of us.

We might not have been the closest family, but in those months, we proved that when it really mattered, we could come together. Even if it was over expired tuna and broken showers.

The Estate Sale Spectacle

We organized an estate sale and auction, transforming the house into a chaotic marketplace for a weekend. Neighbors, strangers, and even a local collector of vintage typewriters descended upon the house to sift through decades of accumulated possessions. Every item seemed to have a story, whether it was Dad's prized but entirely nonfunctional coffee grinder or the set of mismatched chairs we lovingly referred to as the "wobblers."

In the end, we managed to clear out a significant amount and marveled at what people were willing to buy. Whatever didn't sell was taken away by the auction company, and we donated several truckloads of items to charity.

A Bittersweet Victory

All the work paid off as the house was sold in the first week it was on the market, much to everyone's relief. After months of relentless cleaning, repairs, and organizing, the speed of the sale felt like a small miracle. The realtor credited the quick turnaround to the updated fixtures, decluttered spaces, and Jason's hard work in coordinating contractors to make the house shine. We all shared a mix of pride and exhaustion, knowing the effort had not only restored the house but also brought us closer as a family—even if only temporarily.

After much deliberation and some delicate negotiations, we managed to convince Dad to move into assisted living. Jen, Trish, and Dawn took charge of the mission, visiting multiple facilities and debating their merits like reality show judges. After several tours and consultations, the team settled on a cozy, well-reviewed place near the house in Ashburn, VA. The deciding factor? The facility's flexibility: they only required a 30-day notice to move out. This gave Dad the illusion of control and us a lifeline if things didn't work out. The place also had amenities like a garden and common areas that we hoped would soften the blow. It wasn't easy, but we were cautiously optimistic that this arrangement would work.

Selling the house of a loved one with Lewy Body Dementia requires sensitivity, careful planning, and clear communication. Begin by involving all relevant family members to ensure a unified approach and minimize conflict. Consult the person with dementia if possible, respecting their autonomy and including them in decisions. Secure legal authority, such as power of attorney, if necessary, to manage the sale. Declutter and depersonalize the home to make it appealing to potential buyers while preserving keepsakes that hold sentimental value. Work with a trusted real estate agent who understands the unique challenges of selling a home under these circumstances. Set realistic expectations for pricing and timeline, considering market conditions. Use proceeds from the sale strategically, aligning with the individual's care needs; for example, use the funds for transitioning to assisted living or covering medical expenses. Keep open communication with all involved to navigate the process smoothly and ensure decisions prioritize the well-being and dignity of your loved one.

ESCAPE FROM THE LOCKUP

After staying at the assisted living facility for a only short while, Dad felt like every day was the same dull routine. The confusion of dementia had taken hold of his mind, and he couldn't shake the feeling that he was trapped in some sort of prison. It didn't help that the doors were always locked, the staff was always hovering, and the walls were too high to climb over. Dad was no fool—he knew something was off, and he wasn't going to sit idly by while the world outside moved on without him.

One sunny afternoon, Dad had had enough. The staff were distracted, so he decided to make his escape. He approached the front door with a sense of urgency and confidence, ready to bust free. But just as he reached for the handle, Nurse Julie appeared out of nowhere like a guard dog.

"Tim, where do you think you're going?" she asked, raising an eyebrow.

"I'm going for a walk," Dad replied, puffing out his chest like a prisoner granted a rare moment of freedom.

Julie smiled politely. "You know you can't leave, Mr. Porter."

His face twisted into a scowl. "What do you mean I can't leave? I'm not a prisoner!"

Dad tried to push past her, but Nurse Julie was quick, holding the door firmly. "Sorry, Mr. Porter, rules are rules." The entire staff formed a wall, creating an impenetrable barrier.

Dad's frustration built like a pressure cooker, and soon he was shouting, "Let me out! I need to get out of here!"

Nurse Julie stepped aside and spoke in a soothing voice. "Tim, I know you're upset, but yelling won't help. Let's take a few deep breaths, okay?"

Dad, still fuming, sighed and reluctantly backed down. He was not giving up, though. He'd find another way out. The staff could not keep him cooped up forever!

Later that afternoon, the family received a call. The facility explained that Dad's aggressive outbursts were unacceptable and that it would be best to hire someone to stay with him until he could be moved to the Memory Care unit. Reluctantly, we agreed to hire a sitter to keep an eye on him. His sitter, Rose, was a kind-hearted young woman with a patient demeanor, but Dad wasn't too concerned with that right now.

Dad immediately began to plot. The front desk always had coffee brewing–Dad knew that's where he could make his move. He needed a plan. So, he worked on Rose.

"Hey, Rose," Dad said, flashing his most charming grin. "Wouldn't it be nice if you had just one more cup of coffee?"

Rose yawned. "Sure, Tim. I could use a little caffeine boost."

Dad grinned mischievously. "I'll have a cup too," he said, handing Rose his empty coffee mug. "You should drink it all—real fast."

Rose nodded, oblivious, and started gulping down the coffee as Dad waited patiently. Then, when she went to the bathroom, Dad made his move. He approached the front desk with a casual stride. "Hey, you're out of coffee," he said.

The attendant, already accustomed to such requests, walked around the corner to brew another batch. This was Dad's chance. As soon as the attendant was out of sight, Dad shuffled out the door as quickly as his feet would carry him.

The cool, fresh air outside felt like freedom. He wasn't sure where he was going, but he was going somewhere! Dad wandered down the path, his heart racing with the thrill of rebellion, until he spotted a school bus where kids were loading up for their ride to school. This was it—his big break!

Dad hurried over to the bus and raised his hands dramatically. "Excuse me, kids!" he said loudly. "I've been abducted! Can one of you please call the police?"

The kids stared at him with wide eyes, unsure of how to react. One brave student finally stepped forward. "The police station is just across the street," the kid said, pointing.

Dad nodded with urgency. "Yes! That's it! The police will help me!"

With newfound determination, Dad marched across the street and into the police station. He approached the officer at the front desk, who looked up at him with a mix of curiosity and concern.

"I've been abducted," Dad said seriously.

The officer raised an eyebrow but smiled kindly. "Well, let's get to the bottom of this. Who took you?"

"I live at that place over there," Dad said, pointing back toward the assisted living facility. "They won't let me leave. I need to get out!"

The officer nodded sympathetically and immediately called my sister Trish. Trish explained everything to the police, and soon enough, the staff from the assisted living facility arrived to escort Dad back.

Back inside the facility, Dad was still brimming with rebellious energy. He looked around, scanning for his next opportunity. And then, he spotted it: the fire alarm.

With the stealth of a seasoned escape artist, Dad pulled the alarm. The blaring sound filled the building, sending the staff into a frenzy to manage the chaos.

"That's it!" Dad muttered to himself. "No one's keeping me locked up"

But it wasn't long before the facility staff took their next action. They moved Dad into the Memory Care unit, where the walls were just a little higher, and the doors were just a little firmer. The space was quieter, the staff more attentive, and the exits more elusive.

Dad, however, wasn't finished yet. As he sat down in his new room, his mind began to whirl with new possibilities. He smiled to himself, a glimmer of determination in his eye. "It's just a matter of time," he muttered. "Just a matter of time."

Finding an assisted living facility for a physically active parent with dementia can be a delicate balancing act. It's essential to prioritize both their cognitive needs and their physical well-being. Start by researching facilities that specialize in memory care, as these are often better equipped to handle the unique challenges of dementia. When evaluating options, look for programs that encourage physical activity, such as daily exercise classes, walking groups, or access to secure outdoor spaces. Tour the facilities to observe how they cater to active residents and ensure their safety, such as using enclosed courtyards or monitoring systems.

Additionally, speak with the staff members to understand their approach to balancing independence with supervision—ensuring your parent has the freedom to move while remaining safe from risks associated with wandering or accidents. Consider the social aspect as well; facilities with group activities and opportunities for interaction can help maintain your parent's sense of purpose and engagement. Finally, involve your parent in the decision-making process as much as possible. While their cognitive challenges may limit their ability to fully comprehend the situation, giving them some say can help ease the transition.

TIM TAKES ON MEMORY CARE

Moving to the Memory Care unit of Sunny Days Assisted Living wasn't exactly on Dad's bucket list. Sure, the staff was friendly enough, and the food wasn't half bad (if you liked variations on beige), but the decor—a mix of faux flowers and faded wallpaper—screamed "we've given up on excitement." For Dad, a man who could still swing a 9-iron and occasionally remember where his ball landed, the place felt like a mismatch.

Dad was the odd duck in a pond full of slowly paddling mallards. Most of the other residents were either rolling around in wheelchairs or hunched over walkers that groaned with every shuffle. Meanwhile, Dad could still stroll confidently, occasionally breaking into a jog just to prove a point. The staff called him "Spry Tim," which he took as a compliment (though he preferred "Tim the Terrific").

His saving grace was the sitter service he'd kept from his pre-Memory Care days. She provided companionship, a buffer against the sometimes-bewildering blur of faces and activities. His sitter became his sidekick—or, as Dad put it, "my personal referee in the game of life."

Pee-per Trails and Quick Reflexes

One Tuesday afternoon, Dad found himself in the middle of what he would later refer to as "The Great Hallway

Flood." Two residents, both in wheelchairs, had misjudged their timing and left puddles of urine in the corridor. Dad, ever alert, executed a maneuver that would've made a ninja proud. With a hop, a skip, and a yelp, he managed to avoid the incoming streams of urine entirely. He darted behind Rose, using her as a human shield, and exclaimed, "Call the Coast Guard, it's a flash flood!"

Rose, shaking her head with she handed him a towel. "You're supposed to protect me, not the other way around!" she quipped.

"Hey, you're the professional here!" Dad shot back, grinning as he wiped his shoes. "And this was a tactical retreat."

Later that day, Dad told anyone who would listen about his daring escape. The story grew with each retelling, until it sounded like he'd narrowly escaped a tsunami. "You wouldn't believe the speed and precision it took," he said to one of the attendants, who nodded indulgently.

The Great Escape

A few days later, Dad decided he'd had enough of Memory Care. He was moving out. Where? He wasn't sure. But he'd packed his bags. Every single piece of clothing he owned was folded (sort of) and stacked in the hallway outside his room.

When the staff found him, Dad was sitting triumphantly on his suitcase, waiting for his nonexistent getaway car.

"Where are you going, Dad?" I asked over the phone, summoned by the flustered staff.

"Anywhere but here! I've got my golf clubs ready," Dad declared.

"You're not moving out," I said with a tone that blended exasperation and affection. "You can't just move your stuff into the hallway. Now, please behave yourself and unpack."

Dad grumbled but complied, muttering about how even Alcatraz had better escape plans. He turned the event into a comedic saga, telling everyone how "the warden" (aka me) had foiled his bid for freedom.

Ashley and the Drug Dealers

For a couple of weeks, Dad was convinced his wife, Ashley, had flown in from China to be with him. The only hitch? She'd been abducted by drug dealers. He was sure of it. He hallucinated a gang of people grabbing her and shoving her into their car, their faces shadowed and menacing as they sped away into the night.

One night, Dad thought he saw her sleeping on his bed, and he absolutely refused to sleep, convinced she needed his protection from unseen dangers. Despite Rose and the staff's best efforts to reassure him, Dad remained steadfast, pacing the room and muttering about kidnappers.

Finally, I came up with what I thought was a creative solution. "Dad, why don't you try touching her? If she's real, you'll know," I suggested over the phone.

Dad reached out, his hand slicing through empty air. He blinked, confused. "She's gone," he whispered. Then, with a shrug, he climbed into bed and promptly fell asleep.

The next morning, he told Rose, "Guess Ashley's handling those drug dealers herself. She's a tough cookie."

Life Goes On

Though Dad didn't exactly blend into the Memory Care crowd, he brought a certain zest to the place. Whether he was dodging puddles, planning escapes, or solving imaginary kidnappings, he kept the staff on its toes and the other residents entertained.

One afternoon, he strolled into the activity room and announced, "If anyone's interested in poker, I'll be at table two. Loser buys the pudding cups." He had no takers, but still spent the afternoon shuffling cards and telling stories about his "glory days" on the golf course or in the Navy.

"You know," he said to Rose one afternoon, "this place isn't half bad. But if they ever start serving green Jell-O, I'm out of here."

Assisted living and memory care are two types of long-term care designed to support individuals with different needs. Assisted living primarily serves seniors who are relatively independent but need help with daily activities such as bathing, dressing, medication management, or meal preparation. These communities often provide private apartments, social activities, and opportunities for independence in a supportive environment. Memory care, on the other hand, is a specialized type of assisted living tailored to individuals with Alzheimer's disease, dementia, or other cognitive impairments. It features secured environments to prevent wandering, staff trained in dementia care, and programs designed to enhance cognitive function and provide structure. While both options offer support, memory care emphasizes safety and tailored care for cognitive challenges, making it ideal for individuals with more advanced memory-related needs.

ADVENTURES IN DOCTORLAND

For most people, a trip to the doctor is a straightforward affair. You show up, you list your symptoms, and you listen to the doctor tell you what's wrong with you. For our dad, though, doctor visits were less a matter of routine and more an epic quest — with a healthy dose of improvisational theater and a dash of chaos.

"Are you ready, Dad?" one of us would ask before an appointment, clipboard and notebook in hand like we were preparing for a UN briefing.

"Of course! I'm feeling great. Let's do this," he'd reply with the confidence of a man about to charm the pants off his general practitioner. Therein lay the problem: "feeling great" didn't always match up with the facts.

The doctor would ask, "So, how's your balance? Any falls lately?" And Dad, with his trademark grin, would wave each fall off like he'd just tripped over a pebble in the driveway. Meanwhile, whoever joined him for that visit was frantically miming no, no, no from the sidelines, knowing full well that he'd fallen twice last week—once while trying to swat a fly with a rolled-up magazine and another time while attempting to "fix" the garden hose by wrestling it like a python.

Then there were the virtual appointments. Oh, those were a special kind of chaos. Imagine trying to coax an honest health assessment out of someone who has discovered the mute button but refuses to admit it. "Dad, they can't hear you," Jen would say, her frustration rising. Meanwhile, Dad's face would be inches from the camera as he pretended not to understand technology... except he knew exactly what he was doing.

On good days, he'd at least try to give the doctor something resembling an accurate report. But more often than not, he would spin his own version of events.

"How are you sleeping, Tim?" the doctor might ask.

"Oh, like a baby," Dad would respond confidently.

Jen, Jason, or I would have to chime in with the truth: "Actually, he was up at three a.m. making a snack, at five a.m. rearranging the kitchen cabinets, and at six thirty he decided the vacuum needed some exercise."

Dad's version of the LBD diagnosis was far from the truth. Once, after a particularly long appointment, he came home and announced, "The doctor said I'm doing better than anyone they've ever seen with this... Lewy Dewy, or whatever it's called again?"

"Lewy Body Dementia, Dad," I reminded him.

"Right, that. Well, apparently I'm their star patient. They're calling me the poster boy!"

What the doctor actually said was, "We're monitoring your symptoms, and there's no significant improvement. Stay consistent with your medications." But Dad's optimism (or denial) was like a runaway train: once it got going, there was no stopping it.

The toughest part for all of us was that Dad didn't fully grasp the gravity of his diagnosis.

"So, this thing I have," he'd say, usually while stirring his coffee. "It'll go away eventually, right?"

"No, Dad," we'd explain gently. "It's progressive. It's going to get worse over time."

"Well, that's just silly," he'd reply, shrugging it off as if we were talking about a minor inconvenience like a broken toaster. And then he'd change the subject: "Have you tried these bagels? They're amazing."

Dad would sometimes ask about research studies, hopeful that somewhere out there a breakthrough was just around the corner. He would also casually plan the things he'd do "when this is all over," as though Lewy Body Dementia was just a temporary detour on the road of life. One recurring dream of his involved taking a Flying Scot sailboat out on the lake, gliding effortlessly across the water. "You kids can join if you like, but you'll have to keep up," he teased, as if he was preparing for the Olympics. It didn't matter that he hadn't been on a boat in years; in his mind, the wind was always just right, and the horizon stretched endlessly ahead. Sometimes he'd go into elaborate detail, describing the pristine white sails and the sound of water lapping against the hull. "The doctor said I'll be back at it in no time," he'd insist, despite no such conversation having occurred.

There were moments when his humor was disarming. "Look, if this thing gives me an excuse to forget your birthdays, I'm all for it," he joked once. But beneath the jokes was the heartbreaking reality that we all knew but didn't want to say out loud. Lewy Body Dementia had no cure. The treatments available were, at best, lukewarm band-aids on a leaky faucet. And the life expectancy... well, its only 3-5 years.

Jason, Jen, and I took turns going to the appointments, sharing the emotional load and swapping notes on Dad's ever-evolving narratives. We became experts at managing expectations and translating Dad's exaggerations into actionable updates. By the end of each visit, it felt less like we'd gone to a doctor and more like we'd unraveled a complex puzzle.

In the end, though, those adventures in Doctorland weren't just about the medical updates or the missed details. They were about navigating this absurd, painful, and sometimes hilarious journey with Dad as our unflappable captain, steering the ship straight into uncharted waters with a grin on his face and a "poster boy" badge pinned firmly to his chest. And if he could, he'd steer that ship right onto the deck of his Flying Scot, ready for one last race against the horizon.

Taking a loved one with dementia to the doctor requires careful preparation and patience to ensure the visit is productive and minimize the stress for everyone involved. Start by planning ahead—make a list of symptoms, behaviors, or concerns to discuss, as well as any medications your loved one is taking. Bring along any necessary documentation, such as medical history or advanced directives. Arrive early to allow time for everyone to settle, as rushing can increase anxiety. During the visit, use clear and simple language, and be prepared to act as your loved one's advocate if they struggle to communicate. Stay calm and supportive, especially if they become confused or agitated. It's also helpful to inform the doctor of your loved one's preferences and routines to make the experience more comfortable for them. After the appointment, recap the visit with the doctor's recommendations and make adjustments to the care plan as needed. Remember, empathy, patience, and preparation can make a significant difference in navigating these appointments effectively.

THE GREAT NAME DEBATE

The rhythmic hum of the car wheels on the highway and the low murmur of the radio created a soothing atmosphere. I was focused on driving, one hand lightly gripping the steering wheel while the other adjusted the air conditioning vent. Dad sat slumped in the passenger seat, his head tilted forward, snoring softly. It was one of those rare, serene moments in an otherwise difficult drive. As with most things involving Dad these days, serenity was fleeting.

"Hey!" Dad suddenly exclaimed, snapping awake. His eyes darted around, disoriented. "Where am I?"

"You're in the car, Dad," I replied, glancing over briefly before returning my eyes to the road.

Dad squinted at me, tilting his head like a curious bird. "Who are you?"

I sighed inwardly. "It's me, Dad. Tim."

"Tim?" Dad repeated, his brow furrowing. "That's my name."

"I know," I said, bracing myself for an interesting conversation. "I'm Tim too."

"No, you're not!" Dad said, crossing his arms and giving me a suspicious look. "Why would there be two Tims in one family? That's just... ridiculous."

"You named me after you," I said.

Dad shook his head. "Nope. Wouldn't have done that. Doesn't sound like me."

"Well, you did."

Dad leaned closer, scrutinizing his son's face. "You look familiar. You've got the family nose, but you're not a Tim. Are you David?"

"No, Dad," I said, stifling a laugh. "David's your brother. And no offense, but I look nothing like him."

"Hmm," Dad mused, sitting back and scratching his chin. "You've got the same look as David. Could've sworn... But two Tims? That's just confusing. Whose idea was that?"

"Yours," I said, my voice tinged with both amusement and exasperation.

"Nope. Don't buy it," Dad said, shaking like a human bobblehead. "Why would I name you Tim? That's lazy. It's like wearing the same shirt as someone else to a family reunion. Awkward."

I laughed. "Well, I'm named after you because—"

"Because what?" Dad interrupted. "I lost a bet?"

"No, because Mom thought it would be nice to name me after you."

Dad scoffed. "Nice? She must've been having a bad day. If it were up to me, I'd have done it differently."

"Oh yeah? How would you have named me?"

"Easy," Dad said confidently, as if the answer was obvious. "I'd make a list of all the names in the family and pick the first one that wasn't already taken."

"That sounds... efficient," I said, "Alright, what would you have picked?"

Dad rubbed his chin, deep in thought. "Okay, let's see. There's David, obviously. Then there's Mike and... uh, Joe. Nope."

"Go on," I urged, intrigued.

"Oh! Albert!" Dad exclaimed, his face lighting up. "Albert isn't taken. I'd have named you Albert."

I burst out laughing. "Albert?"

"Yeah!" Dad said indignantly. "It's a solid name. You could've been an Al. Or Bert. People like a good Bert."

"Bert," I repeated, shaking my head. "You're kidding, right?"

"Nope!" Dad declared, crossing his arms triumphantly. "You'd make a great Albert. Better than two Tims running around causing confusion."

I grinned, shaking my head as we continued driving. "Well, sorry to disappoint you, Dad. But I'm sticking with Tim."

"Suit yourself," Dad muttered, settling back into his seat. "But don't come crying to me when people can't tell us apart."

The car was quiet again, except for the soft hum of the engine. I glanced over and saw Dad's eyes slowly closing. But just as I thought the conversation was over, Dad spoke once more.

"Albert," he mumbled, barely audible. "Would've been a damn good name..."

I chuckled, my laughter mingling with the soft snores from the passenger seat. Moments like these made every journey with Dad memorable. I couldn't resist mulling over the name Albert. What if he really had named me Albert? Would I have been more distinguished? A math professor? Or maybe a jazz musician? It was funny how a name could carry so much weight, though in their family, it seemed humor carried even more.

As the car continued down the highway, Dad woke up again, this time blinking at the passing landscape. "You know," he started, his voice a little scratchy from his nap, "Albert would've gone well with our last name. Albert… What's your last name again?"

"It's Porter, Dad. Same as yours."

"Oh, right, right," Dad said, nodding sagely.

And with that, Dad settled back into his seat, drifting off to sleep once more. I couldn't stop smiling as we drove, the echoes of our playful banter lingering in the air. Sometimes, these odd little conversations made everything feel right—even when everything was confusing.

DAD MOVES TO CHINA

Moving Dad to China was one of those life decisions that sounded ridiculous to everyone at first—including me. After all, who uproots a man battling Lewy Body Dementia and sends him halfway around the world? But once I weighed the pros and cons, the answer was clear. The memory care facility wasn't cutting it. Dad was physically outpacing his peers, and spending time in a room full of people more detached from reality than he was made him restless. Sure, his mind had its moments of fog, but there were still hours where he was the dad I remember… well, mostly.

Ashley had moved back to Shangrao a year earlier. Though she was a bit wary, she seemed willing to take on the role of Dad's primary caregiver. She had worked as an in-home elder care professional before, so she had experience. Plus, Dad had a soft spot for her cooking. If anyone could coax him into living a happier, more grounded existence, it was Ashley with a wok in her hand and a steamer full of dumplings.

Of course, getting Dad to China was about as easy as convincing him that tofu wasn't meat. First, there was the matter of the visa. Jason took the lead on this project, and quickly realized that navigating the Chinese bureaucracy while in the United States was like trying to play chess with someone twelve hours ahead of you. You make a move; they respond in the middle of your night. We needed letters, photos of IDs, and about ten other forms that none of us had ever heard of.

The *pièce de résistance*? The embassy interview. We were all on pins and needles for that one, especially since Dad's hallucinations had a way of creeping in at the worst times. What if he started telling the officer about the talking squirrel that followed him around? Or about how he was secretly running a pirate ship from the memory care unit? But Dad surprised us all, answering every question with the kind of polite clarity he reserved for moments when he wanted something—in this case, to get out of the memory care facility. "I'm moving to China to be with my wife," he said with a grin. The officer stamped his paperwork without a second glance.

Now that the visa was sorted, we turned to the logistics of the move—a whole other beast. Packing for a man with dementia is an exercise in futility. He wanted to bring things he didn't need ("Timmy, we'll need my golf clubs for the trip") and didn't want to bring things he absolutely did ("Why would I need a coat? China's warm!"). I tried to explain that China had winters too, but he waved us off. "Ashley will knit me one if it's cold. She's good at that kind of thing." (For the record, Ashley does not knit). It took multiple rounds of unpacking, repacking, and sneaky editing of his suitcase before we got it down to the essentials.

Then there was the flight. Oh, the flight. Thirteen hours in a pressurized tube with a man who occasionally thought flight attendants were government agents trying to steal his memories? What could possibly go wrong? Jason took Dad by himself, braving the journey with equal parts determination and caffeine. By some miracle, Dad slept through most of the flight, waking up only to announce loudly, "We're flying over Kansas!" (They were over the Pacific.) When they landed in Shanghai, Jason was exhausted, but Dad seemed invigorated, ready to take on his new life.

Ashley met them at the airport with her usual mix of enthusiasm and no-nonsense efficiency. She gave Jason a warm hug, clapped Dad on the back, and immediately began orchestrating the next leg of the journey: a high-speed train ride to Shangrao. The train was a marvel to Dad, who spent the entire trip alternately napping and pressing his face to the window like a child on his first road trip. Ashley patiently explained the sights along the way, from the sprawling rice paddies to the distant mountains, while Dad nodded and exclaimed, "This is better than television!"

The first week was… an adjustment. Dad's internal clock didn't just have jet lag; it had a full-blown identity crisis. He'd be wide awake at 2 a.m., rifling through drawers and muttering about misplaced treasure maps. Ashley, bless her, took it in stride. She'd make him tea and sit with him until he settled down. During the day, she'd take him on walks, where he quickly became a local celebrity. The neighbors adored him, especially when he tried to speak Mandarin, his pronunciation turning even the simplest words into accidental comedy routines.

By the end of the month, Dad seemed more content than he'd been in years. He loved the food, the pace of life, and—most importantly—Ashley's company. They developed a routine: breakfast in the courtyard, a morning walk to the market, and afternoons filled with puzzles or storytelling sessions where Dad would regale Ashley's family with tales from his youth. His favorite part of the day was dinner, a communal affair filled with laughter, chopsticks clicking, and dishes he couldn't pronounce but devoured with gusto.

"Timmy," he said one evening during our regular WhatsApp calls, sounding unusually serious. "Thank you for letting me come here. I think I'm going to like being Chinese."

I didn't have the heart to explain citizenship laws, so I just nodded. "You're doing great, Dad."

Sometimes, the most unlikely decisions turn out to be the best ones.

BIRTH OF THE POWDER EFFECT

The Powder Effect birth happened while Dad was on a trip to the US for Thanksgiving. Dad held his phone as if it were the Holy Grail of modern technology. To him, it wasn't just a phone—it was a lifeline, a digital Swiss Army knife, a tiny magical slab that contained the universe. He treated it with reverence and obsession, rarely letting it out of his sight. So, when the unthinkable happened during a visit to my house, chaos ensued.

It all began on a crisp morning. Jen was enjoying breakfast while I was busy working.

"Where's my phone?" Dad asked, his voice tinged with suspicion, as if accusing the room itself of thievery.

"I'm sure it's around here somewhere," I said, sipping my coffee, while working from home. I later regretted my nonchalance.

But Dad wasn't convinced. "No, it's gone. It's vanished. Disintegrated, maybe. You know, the Powder Effect!"

"The what?" Jen asked, instantly regretting her curiosity.

"The Powder Effect," Dad repeated, wide-eyed. "Sometimes it turns to powder. Then it'll reconstruct itself, but only when it feels like it. That phone has special powers."

Jen and I exchanged wary glances. We knew better than to argue when Dad was in one of his mystical moods.

The hunt began in earnest. Dad tore apart the guest room with the fervor of a treasure hunter digging for gold. The bed was stripped to its skeleton. The bookshelf? Emptied. The closet? Cleared out with the vigor of a hurricane. Jen combed through the rest of the house with the patience of a saint, while I retraced dad's steps for the umpteenth time. Even our 29-year-old son Jonathan was roped into the operation, muttering under his breath about how he could've been gaming instead.

Calling the phone was pointless; the battery was dead, a cruel twist of fate that Dad declared was another manifestation of the Powder Effect.

"You see," he explained as he rummaged through a drawer of mismatched socks, "sometimes the Powder Effect brings the workers. They're the ones who move things around."

"The workers?" Jonathan asked.

"Yes, the workers. Always busy, moving things right under our noses. They're not malicious, just... mischievous."

Two days passed in this frantic search. By the end, the house looked like it had been ransacked by overzealous burglars. Usually immaculate, it now resembled the aftermath of a tornado, and everyone was on edge. Finally, when hope was nearly lost, the phone was discovered—wrapped in a bedspread like some secret artifact.

"The workers must've put it there," Dad said triumphantly. "See? The Powder Effect at work."

The phone was dead, of course, but Dad held it like a long-lost friend, beaming with pride as if he had solved the mystery of the century.

Stairway Mysteries

The stairs were another enigma that plagued Dad during his stay. Every day, without fail, he'd stop in front of Jen or me and ask, "Where are the stairs?" It became common for Dad to wonder how to get to his bedroom, as if the staircase had decided to play hide-and-seek.

"They're right there," Jen would say, pointing to the unmistakable staircase.

Dad would squint at it, unconvinced. "Why would anyone put stairs there? Doesn't make any sense. There's gotta be more stairs somewhere."

Dad would also ask Jen, often with a tone of exasperation, if the house was always going to be in its present configuration. "Why is everything here so... permanent? Are you sure the walls don't move? Or the furniture?" he'd inquire. It was as if he expected the entire house to reconfigure itself overnight. His questions were a mix of genuine curiosity and the kind of whimsical suspicion that made Jen wonder if he thought the house was alive. Every morning, it seemed, the layout was a fresh mystery for Dad to solve.

He spent hours exploring closets and side rooms, convinced that a secret staircase lurked somewhere in the house. Despite daily explanations, the stairs remained a puzzle as vexing as the Powder Effect itself.

Obsessing Over the Wallet and the Green Bag

Dad's phone wasn't his only prized possession. Equally important were his wallet and a small green bag he used to store his medication and important papers. Many times a day, he'd sit down at the foot of his bed or the kitchen counter, carefully unzip the bag, and empty its contents. Each item was scrutinized as if it were part of a sacred inventory.

"Okay, that's the medication," he'd say, lining up the bottles. "And these are the papers." He'd stack them meticulously, only to shuffle through them again minutes later to ensure nothing had mysteriously disappeared. "They're all here," he'd conclude, but within an hour, the ritual would repeat itself.

His wallet underwent a similar inspection. Dad would take out each card, holding them up one by one. "How many cards am I supposed to have?" he'd ask. I would patiently count them with him, confirming the total. Satisfied for a moment, Dad would slip the cards back into the wallet, usually in a different order than before, convinced this new arrangement was how they were always meant to be.

It became a family joke. "Don't worry," Jonathan quipped one day, "if the Powder Effect moves anything, Grandpa'll catch it in the next round of checks."

These habits, while repetitive, offered Dad a sense of control in a world that often felt chaotic and confusing. Watching him, Jen and I couldn't help but admire his determination to keep track of what mattered most to him—even if it meant going through the same motions a dozen times a day. It was a testament to his resilience in the face of the invisible chaos he perceived around him.

Mistaken Identities

Adding to the comedy of errors was Dad's tendency to confuse Jen with his wife, Ashley, who was back home in China. One evening, as everyone was settling down, he approached Jen with a gentle smile.

"Goodnight, dear," he said, leaning in for a kiss.

Jen, quick on her feet, ducked her head slightly so he ended up kissing the top of her head instead of her lips. She managed it with such grace that I was impressed. Dad, none the wiser, shuffled off to bed, content with his affectionate goodbye.

A few days later, things got slightly more awkward when Dad, still mistaking Jen for Ashley, suggested they be intimate, his confusion bringing an uncomfortable energy to the afternoon.

"Dad, Ashley's not here," Jen reminded him gently, redirecting him back to his room. It became another part of the family's growing repertoire of stories, each one tinged with humor, warmth, and the occasional awkward moment.

The Legacy of The Powder Effect

By the time the visit ended, everyone was exhausted but oddly amused. "The Powder Effect" had entered the family's lexicon, becoming the go-to explanation for every lost item or unexplained event. Dad's descriptions of the workers and their mischievous antics became a source of endless jokes and reflections.

We expect that for years to come, Jonathan and the other kids will recount the story to friends, laughing as they describe their grandfather's conviction in the mystical powers of his phone and the busy workers who moved things around. Even the stairs and the green bag inspections will find their way into family anecdotes.

Dad, of course, remained blissfully unaware of the legacy he had created, still convinced that his phone's magic was very real. To him, the world was alive with wonder and mystery—it was a place where phones could disintegrate, stairs could move, and invisible workers could tirelessly reshuffle his belongings. Maybe he wasn't entirely wrong.

Humor can be a powerful tool when caring for someone with dementia, offering moments of connection, relief, and joy in an otherwise challenging journey. As dementia progresses, it can strip away many aspects of a person's independence and identity, but shared laughter can cut through those losses. Humor helps caregivers navigate difficult or awkward situations, such as repeated questions or unexpected behaviors, with grace and patience. It can also provide a much-needed emotional release, lightening the weight of stress and preventing burnout. For the person with dementia, laughter can spark moments of clarity, happiness, and comfort, grounding them in the present. While dementia is a serious condition, finding humor in small, everyday moments is not only a coping mechanism but also a way to preserve the humanity and dignity of everyone involved.

MONEY TALKS

If there was one thing that defined my dad, it was his relationship with money. For him, money wasn't just a means to an end. It was his scoreboard, his compass, his constant companion—sometimes more important than his family, if we're being honest. It wasn't just about having enough; it was about having more, always more, even if the pursuit drove everyone else a little crazy.

Growing up, Dad had this habit of bringing money into every conversation, even if it didn't belong there. "All you kids care about is my money!" he once said, exasperated, when one of us wanted a $5 bill for a school book fair. That moment seared itself into my brain. I made it my mission to never rely on his money. I didn't want him thinking I was after his "nest egg"—whatever that even meant. The idea of being financially independent became more than just a goal; it was a point of pride, something to prove to myself and to him.

Fast-forward to the Lewy Body Dementia years, and Dad's tight grip on his finances had turned into a chaotic juggling act. His once-impressive money management skills had morphed into $80,000 in credit card debt, overdue bills, and monthly expenses that looked like they belonged to a Fortune 500 CEO. It became clear that someone needed to step in. And that someone, thanks to a long-ago conversation, was me.

The Reluctant Guardian

Years earlier, while dealing with his prostate cancer diagnosis, Dad asked me to be his guardian if he ever became disabled. I was shocked. We hadn't seen each other in years at that point. Most of our conversations revolved around work or his attempts to recruit me as a guest speaker for his university classes. I reluctantly agreed, thinking it was just a precaution. A lawyer drafted the paperwork, and that was that. Little did I know how this agreement would one day drag me into a labyrinth of financial chaos.

When LBD took hold, I inherited a new job: managing Dad's money. It started with spreadsheets—glorious, color-coded spreadsheets. I outlined every bill, expense, and potential cost of care, projecting scenarios for the next two to ten years. I even reviewed these spreadsheets with Dad—15 to 20 times in two days on one trip to Northern Virginia. He'd stare at the numbers like they were written in hieroglyphs. "But where's the rest of it?" he'd ask, genuinely baffled.

"Dad, this is the rest of it."

He'd shake his head, unconvinced. "It just doesn't seem right," he'd mutter, staring suspiciously at the neatly aligned columns and rows. The man who once balanced complex investment portfolios now struggled to grasp even the basics of his finances. It was heartbreaking and maddening all at once.

Midnight Money Madness

Once I took over the accounts, the phone calls began. He'd ring me up five times a day, sometimes at ungodly hours, to ask about his account balances. "How much money do I have again?" he'd say, as if he were calling to check on a pizza delivery. But he rarely remembered how many accounts he actually had or how much was supposed to be in them. Hallucinations didn't help; sometimes he'd accuse imaginary people of stealing his money. Once, at 3 a.m., he called to inform me that a mysterious "they" had siphoned off his savings.

"Who's they, Dad?"

"You know... them! The ones who want it all."

In the early days, Dad still had access to his accounts, which was... less than ideal. He'd forget passwords, lock himself out, change the password, and then promptly forget the new one. This vicious cycle of account lockouts became a biweekly event. Sometimes, I felt more like a tech support agent than a son. I'd spend hours on the phone with banks, untangling his financial messes while he sat on the phone or nearby, alternately apologetic and defiant.

China, Wires, and the Great Bank Debacle

The most ridiculous chapter in this saga unfolded after Dad moved to China with Ashley. I was responsible for wiring money to them monthly. Before he left, we visited a bank branch to ensure I could send funds without issue. Armed with a power of attorney, we were assured that everything was set. But it wasn't.

One day, when trying to wire money, the bank told me I wasn't authorized. Apparently, they thought I was impersonating Dad and promptly locked the account. Since we share the same name, confusion was inevitable, but the timing couldn't have been worse. I ended up sending money from my own account to cover their living expenses. Meanwhile, Dad would call from China, confused and increasingly frustrated. "Why don't you just fix it?" he'd ask, as if I hadn't spent hours navigating the bureaucratic maze.

When Dad came back to the U.S. for a visit (a whole adventure in itself), we unlocked the account and set me up as a joint account holder. This time, we quadruple-checked every form and process, determined not to repeat the debacle. Lesson learned: power of attorney is not the financial cheat code you think it is. It's a mildly useful tool that only works when the stars align and Mercury isn't in retrograde.

Lessons from the Trenches

Managing Dad's finances during the LBD years taught me more than I ever wanted to know about elder care and money. If there's one piece of advice I can offer, it's this: start the money conversation early. No one wants to talk about end-of-life planning, but trust me, it's easier than untangling a web of locked accounts, forgotten passwords, and imaginary financial conspiracies. Have those awkward discussions before the situation becomes an emergency.

For Dad, money may have been an obsession, but in those later years, it became something more. It wasn't just numbers on a spreadsheet: it was the thread that kept us talking. Even when the conversations were repetitive or downright frustrating, they kept us connected.

Sometimes, in the middle of one of those 3 a.m. calls, I'd find myself chuckling despite the exhaustion. "Dad, you have enough," I'd say, and for a brief moment, he'd sound satisfied. "Okay," he'd reply, his voice softening. "That's good to know." And for all the chaos, those moments made it worth it.

The Practical Side

Managing finances for my dad has required careful planning, clear communication, and protective measures to ensure his financial security and prevent exploitation. The first step for us was to assess his current financial situation. We identified all his bank accounts, investments, debts, insurance policies, and other assets. We also reviewed his monthly income sources, like Social Security and his retirement accounts, along with his regular expenses. Luckily, we found that some legal documents, such as his will, trust, and power of attorney (POA), were already in place.

Establishing legal authority became a priority. Years ago, my dad had asked me to be both his financial and medical POA, which gave me the legal authority to manage his finances and make healthcare decisions if he became unable to do so. While he would still be able to make some decisions in this scenario, I also consulted with a law firm to understand the steps necessary to establish legal guardianship in case his condition advanced further.

We also took steps to simplify his financial affairs. We consolidated accounts, set up automatic bill payments, and made sure all his income was deposited directly into his bank account. Regular monitoring of his bank and credit card statements became a routine for us to catch any suspicious activity early. To protect him further, we talked to him about common scams and even considered a credit freeze to prevent unauthorized accounts from being opened in his name.

Planning for long-term care costs was another important step. We explored options like Medicaid, veterans' benefits, and local elder services. While my dad didn't have long-term care insurance, for those who do, it's important to review the policy and understand the benefits.

Updating my dad's estate planning documents was also part of the process. We reviewed his will, trust, and beneficiary designations to make sure they reflected his current wishes. We added advance directives, such as a healthcare POA and living will, so his medical decisions would be clear in the future. Keeping detailed records of all transactions and maintaining documentation, like receipts, bank statements, and legal papers, has been important for transparency and accountability.

THE FAMILY CORPORATION

Our dad had always been a quirky guy, but Lewy Body Dementia took his imagination and cranked it up to eleven. His brain decided to rebrand our family as a Fortune 500 corporation. Forget holidays and hugs—we were now officially "The Company," and everyone had their role. Titles were assigned, job descriptions invented, and a hierarchy was firmly established. For Dad, it all made perfect sense.

Dawn, who had been tirelessly researching Dad's medical care, became "The Research Analyst." According to Dad, she was hired on a generous salary (we never saw a paycheck, though) to evaluate "healthcare vendors and operational efficiencies." Her late-night Googling? That wasn't just concern for Dad's health; it was her professional duty. She was always on a deadline, and presented her findings to the Board of Directors (aka the rest of us).

Jason, who often drove Dad to appointments or to get ice cream (his favorite activity), was assigned the role of "The Driver." But in Dad's eyes, Jason wasn't just any driver. Oh no. He was a top-tier chauffeur who probably wore a little cap and opened the car door with a bow. He managed the fleet (our one aging minivan) with precision and punctuality, keeping operations running smoothly.

Claire, being the youngest, got off easy. She didn't have a specific title so much as she was seen as the cheerful intern—always fetching things, assisting on minor tasks, and enthusiastically learning the ropes. Of course, in Dad's corporate vision, she was still "on probation," and her responsibilities were subject to expansion pending further performance reviews.

Trish, with her knack for organizing and planning, became "Operations Manager." Dad was convinced she kept The Company running smoothly, from scheduling meetings (family dinners) to executing large-scale initiatives (holiday shopping). Her command of spreadsheets and lists impressed even Dad, who occasionally referred to her as "indispensable to the organization's success."

And then there was me. Somehow, I got promoted straight to the top. According to Dad, I was the President, CEO, and general big shot of the entire operation. If anything went wrong—a missing sock, a late dinner, a failed attempt to fix the remote—it was on me. "Albert," he'd say with a stern look, "your company's standards are slipping." I had no idea how I'd ended up in charge, but there I was, trying to steer this ship while everyone else played along.

At first, we tried correcting him. "Dad, we're your family, not a company," we'd insist. But the more we pushed, the more insistent he became. "Nonsense," he'd say. "This is a very well-organized enterprise. Everyone knows their role. We're just missing a quarterly report."

Eventually, we leaned into it. Dawn started referring to her medical research as "updating the project scope." Jason would tip an imaginary hat when chauffeuring him around. Once, when Claire brought him his slippers, she handed them over with a cheery, "Your two o'clock delivery, sir." Trish began setting out detailed agendas for family gatherings, complete with bullet points and action items, just to stay on Dad's good side.

It wasn't always easy to laugh about it. The reality of his condition was always looming in the background. But those moments—when he'd ask Jason if "The Company's fleet vehicle" was washed, or when he'd tell Trish that the holiday party (Christmas) better come in under budget—gave us something to hold onto. They reminded us that even as Dad's mind changed, he was still our dad, still finding a way to organize the chaos in his head.

Dad's fascination with structure wasn't entirely new. He was a workaholic earlier in life, and much of his self-worth and identity were deeply tied to his career. He worked in IT for a large defense contractor, thriving on managing complex projects and ensuring massive deliverables were met on time. He took immense pride in his ability to oversee large engagements, finding both purpose and satisfaction in his role. However, his dedication came at a significant cost. By the time I turned 21, he had missed 17 of my birthdays—sometimes because of work travel, and in his earlier years, due to his service in the Navy.

Looking back, I think this singular focus on work and structure is what ultimately led him to reimagine the family as "The Company" during his later years. It was a way to mirror the organized world he had always known. The titles, the roles, the hierarchy—it was all familiar, perhaps comforting, to him. It gave him a framework to navigate a reality that was increasingly slipping away.

By the end of each day, the CEO (that's me) would often sit back, exhausted but amused. Running a corporation is hard work, especially when your employees think the office is a living room and the quarterly earnings are based on how many scoops of ice cream Dad had. But in the end, The Company kept running—because that's what families do. We adapt, we persevere, and we find humor in the hardest of times. Everyone's contributions mattered—that's what made it home.

Dementia patients often experience a phenomenon known as "time shifting," in which they revert to earlier periods in their lives, recalling themes, people, and events that held significance during those times. This tendency is thought to arise because dementia typically affects short-term memory more acutely than long-term memory, leaving older memories more intact. For many, this manifests in vivid recollections of childhood, early adulthood, or key milestones like a career, military service, or raising children. These memories can feel more real to them than present-day events, influencing their behavior and conversations. For instance, they might speak about long-deceased relatives as though they were still alive or express a strong desire to "go home," referring to a childhood house. The themes they revisit often center around their identity and sense of purpose, such as their role as a parent, a provider, or a caregiver. These moments of connection to the past can offer insights into their emotional needs and provide caregivers with opportunities to engage through reminiscence, helping to create a sense of comfort in an otherwise disorienting world.

BENEFITS

Dad's attempt to get additional coverage from the Veterans Administration was a chapter in his journey that reflected both his determination and the maddening bureaucracy that often accompanies such efforts. With Medicare and supplemental insurance covering only so much of Dad's extensive medical needs, we had to explore every possible avenue to ease the financial burden.

Dawn took on the daunting task of navigating Dad's medical coverage. Whether she got the job because of her aptitude for research or because her husband is a doctor, she embraced the responsibility. She also enlisted Jen, whose knack for organization and thoroughness made her a natural ally. Together, they became the point team for an effort that felt both hopeful and Sisyphean.

Dad served in the Navy during the Vietnam War, a time when countless service members were exposed to harmful chemicals, including Agent Orange. Stories abounded of veterans who had successfully obtained disability and medical coverage for illnesses linked to their military service, and it gave us hope. Parkinson's Disease, in particular, was a condition explicitly tied to Agent Orange exposure in many VA claims. With Dad's Lewy Body Dementia sharing symptoms with Parkinson's, it seemed worth pursuing.

Jen found a local organization specializing in helping veterans navigate the complex VA benefits process. It was a small, scrappy outfit run by people who seemed to genuinely care about helping veterans. They guided us through the process of compiling records, filling out forms, and ensuring that every detail was airtight. But even with their help, the process was daunting.

Dad's stories from his Navy days became a staple of our conversations during this time. Almost daily, he'd recount how his ship would dock at Camp Lejeune to pick up Marines for practice maneuvers. Occasionally, he'd lower his voice to share more thrilling tales of their missions in Vietnam. These stories were vivid and often tinged with pride, but they became bittersweet as the obstacles to proving his claims mounted.

The major issue lay in the nature of Dad's service. Much of his work had been on submarines and involved classified operations. This made it nearly impossible to provide the documentation the VA required to confirm his presence in locations linked to toxic exposures. Despite Dad's earnest testimony and the compelling circumstantial evidence, the lack of concrete proof was an insurmountable barrier.

Dad's determination never wavered, but the process took a toll on all of us. Each setback was a reminder of how much the system could fail the very people it was supposed to serve. In the end, we never secured the coverage. Medicare and out-of-pocket expenses remained our primary resources, leaving us to bear the financial and emotional weight as best we could.

Looking back, the experience was both a lesson in resilience and a stark reminder of the challenges many veterans face. Dad's pride in his service, symbolized by the Navy hat he wore almost every day, never diminished, even as the system seemed to turn a blind eye to the sacrifices he and others had made. And while we didn't achieve the outcome we hoped for, the effort itself was a testament to our family's resolve to honor Dad's service and ensure he received the care he deserved.

Jen took Dad to Richard's Coffee Shop, a vibrant community hub and local service center for veterans. Every Thursday was "Veterans Day" at the coffee shop, a time when the place buzzed with camaraderie and stories of service. Dad beamed with pride when Jen accompanied him to sign the Book of Honor—a cherished tradition in which every visiting veteran's name and branch of service is recorded. As the bell rang and Tim Porter, United States Navy" was called out. Dad's face lit up. It was a moment of recognition that clearly meant the world to him. After just one visit, Dad became captivated by the sense of belonging and made it clear to us that someone had to take him back the following week. Richard's quickly became more than a coffee shop; it was a place where Dad could reconnect with his identity as a veteran and share in a community that valued his service.

When managing insurance coverage for someone with dementia, it's crucial to take proactive steps to ensure medical and long-term care needs are met. Start by reviewing all existing insurance policies, including health, life, and long-term care insurance, to understand the coverage and limitations. Confirm that the person is enrolled in Medicare or Medicaid, as these programs often cover essential services like doctor visits, medications, and hospital stays. Explore supplemental insurance plans if gaps in coverage exist. For long-term care, check if there is an active policy that covers in-home care, assisted living, or nursing home expenses. If no such coverage exists, research Medicaid eligibility, as it may be the primary option for funding long-term care. Notify the insurance companies about the dementia diagnosis to ensure proper documentation and coverage of claims. Consider appointing a durable power of attorney or guardian to handle financial and insurance matters, ensuring bills are paid on time and appeals are made when claims are denied. Regularly reassess the person's needs and update policies accordingly. It can also be helpful to consult with a professional, such as an elder care attorney or insurance specialist.

CATHERINE: A TALE OF RESILIENCE AND LOVE

At 77, my mom, Catherine Porter, is the picture of graceful aging. Active and vibrant, she has always embraced life with an almost boundless energy. Whether kayaking along serene waters, hiking rugged trails, or volunteering at the local soup kitchen, she embodies a zest for life that inspires everyone around her. She is the backbone of our family, a constant source of stability and love, whose presence brings warmth to our lives.

One of Catherine's great passions is hiking–she's tackled some of the world's most storied trails. She hiked the *Camino Francés* with Jonathan, forging memories on that 500-mile pilgrimage that neither will ever forget. Later, she took on the *Camino Português* alongside Jen and our daughter Madison, savoring the beauty and history of Portugal and Spain. Her attempt at the *Camino Inglés* with several of her grandchildren may not have been as successful due to the grandkid's constant bickering, but it still provided stories filled with laughter and lessons that became cherished family lore.

Mom needs to get a hip replacement, a decision that has sparked reflections on her adventures and resilience. Despite the physical toll of hiking iconic trails, she approaches this next step with her characteristic determination. Her decision to move forward with the surgery is less about slowing down and more about preparing for the next chapter, ensuring she can continue the activities she loves and remain the active, vibrant person she's always been.

Her commitment to the community is another defining trait. Volunteering at the local soup kitchen has been a way for her to give back, connecting with people from all walks of life. It's not just about serving meals; it's about showing compassion and understanding to those who need it most.

Mom lives close by and visits our home a few times each week. These visits are always a joy, filled with stories, laughter, and her uncanny ability to make everyone feel loved. The proximity allows us to see firsthand the differences in how she and Dad have aged since their divorce nearly two decades ago. While Mom occasionally repeats a story—a habit that seems harmless compared to the stark challenges of Dad's journey with Lewy Body Dementia—her mind remains sharp.

There's one story that perfectly illustrates the contrast between her mild lapses in memory and Dad's more profound struggles. It involves a birthday card she gave to Jonathan, not once but three years in a row. Jonathan, who has had an interesting diet since childhood—eschewing meat entirely since the age of four and maintaining an unparalleled love for potatoes, especially French fries—received a card from her with a whimsical French fry design. The first year, it was perfect, a playful nod to his unique preferences. The second year, when she gave him the same card, we began to chuckle. By the third year, we wondered if something might be wrong.

It turns out, Mom had loved the card so much that she had bought every copy the store had in stock (she didn't remember how many), intending to use them over time. To her, it wasn't forgetfulness; it was practicality—a sign of how well she knows her grandson and how much she enjoys making him smile. That's Mom: thoughtful in her own quirky way, always putting love into even the smallest gestures.

By contrast, Dad struggles to remember the grandkids' birthdays at all. It's a reminder of how much Lewy Body Dementia has robbed him of, and it makes Mom's steady presence all the more meaningful. While she might tell the same story twice, it's a far cry from "The Workers" or "The Powder Effect," narratives born out of a brain clouded by confusion and delusion. Watching my parents age has been fascinating and, at times, heartbreaking. They started in the same place, but their paths have diverged in ways we never could have anticipated.

Mom's capacity for love, humor, and her unyielding spirit remind us daily of what it means to live fully. In her, we see the strength of a woman who has faced life's challenges head-on, always finding a way to rise above them. While Dad's journey is a struggle, Mom's is a testament to the power of determination, love, and connection.

Mom and Dad hadn't seen each other for many years, but while Dad was visiting from China, his trip happened to coincide with Thanksgiving. My mom, who values family gatherings above all else, decided that having Dad there would not disrupt the tradition. She approached the situation with grace, ensuring the day felt as normal as any other Thanksgiving.

There was a poignant moment when everyone lined up to fill their plates with smoked pork butt, mashed potatoes, sweet potato casserole, and green beans. I stood back and observed the stark contrast between my parents. Mom, vibrant and sharp, was laughing and chatting effortlessly with Jen, the four kids, and me. She moved between conversations, her energy a central force that kept the room warm and lively. Meanwhile, Dad stood apart, his gaze distant, lost in what I can only imagine was the dream world of "The Workers". The juxtaposition was heartbreaking.

AUTHOR'S NOTE

This book began as a few notes to track what was happening with my dad. To my surprise, it evolved into something much more. I hope these stories highlight the beauty in your own life—the laughter and tears that create the meaningful memories and connections we cherish.

APPENDIX

Lewy Body Dementia (LBD) is a complex and challenging neurological disorder that profoundly impacts both individuals living with the condition and their family members. This chapter aims to provide an overview of what LBD is, its symptoms, and its ripple effects on loved ones.

What Is Lewy Body Dementia?

Lewy Body Dementia is the second most common type of progressive dementia after Alzheimer's disease. It is associated with abnormal deposits of a protein called alpha-synuclein in the brain. These deposits, known as Lewy bodies, affect chemicals in the brain, leading to changes in thinking, movement, behavior, and mood. LBD is often divided into two related conditions: Dementia with Lewy Bodies (DLB) and Parkinson's Disease Dementia (PDD). While both involve the presence of Lewy bodies, the key difference lies in the timing and presentation of symptoms. In DLB, cognitive symptoms typically appear before or around the same time as motor symptoms, whereas in PDD, motor symptoms precede cognitive decline by at least a year.

Symptoms and Challenges

LBD presents with a wide range of symptoms that can vary significantly from person to person. The most common symptoms include:

1. Cognitive Impairment:
    a. Problems with attention, executive function, and visual-spatial abilities are often more pronounced than memory loss in the early stages.
    b. Difficulty with problem-solving, planning, and multitasking may emerge early on.
    c. Individuals may struggle with understanding complex concepts or following sequences of instructions.
2. Fluctuating Cognition:
    a. Cognitive abilities may vary widely within a single day or over weeks.
    b. These fluctuations can lead to periods of confusion and/or moments of apparent lucidity, which can be confusing for caregivers.
3. Visual Hallucinations:
    a. Hallucinations are often vivid and detailed: it is common to see, such as seeing animals, people, or objects that are not present.

b. These hallucinations can occur early in the disease and may not cause distress initially, but they can become troubling over time.
4. Parkinsonism:
   a. Symptoms such as tremors, muscle stiffness, slowness of movement (bradykinesia), and difficulty with balance and coordination are common.
   b. Gait disturbances, such as shuffling steps or freezing episodes, can significantly impact mobility and increase fall risk.
5. Sleep Disorders:
   a. Rapid Eye Movement (REM) sleep behavior disorder is a hallmark of LBD. Individuals may act out their dreams, sometimes violently.
   b. Insomnia, excessive daytime sleepiness, and restless leg syndrome are other common sleep-related issues.
6. Autonomic Dysfunction:
   a. Problems with the autonomic nervous system can lead to fluctuations in blood pressure, causing dizziness or fainting.
   b. Other symptoms include constipation, urinary incontinence, and difficulty regulating body temperature.
7. Mood and Behavioral Changes:

- a. Depression, anxiety, and apathy are frequently observed in individuals with LBD.
- b. Behavioral symptoms can include agitation, aggression, delusions, and paranoia, often exacerbating the challenges of caregiving.

8. Sensitivity to Medications:
    - a. People with LBD are often highly sensitive to antipsychotic medications, which can worsen motor symptoms and increase confusion.
    - b. Careful management of medications is critical to avoid adverse effects.

The combination of these symptoms makes LBD particularly challenging to diagnose and manage. Misdiagnosis is common, as symptoms overlap with those of Alzheimer's disease, Parkinson's disease, and psychiatric disorders.

Differences Between LBD and Alzheimer's Disease

Although Lewy Body Dementia and Alzheimer's disease are both forms of dementia, they have distinct differences in symptoms, progression, and treatment approaches:

1. Cognitive Symptoms:

a. In Alzheimer's, memory loss is typically the earliest and most prominent symptom.
   b. In LBD, cognitive decline often begins with issues in attention, problem-solving, and visual-spatial skills, with memory loss appearing later.
2. Hallucinations:
   a. Hallucinations are rare in the early stages of Alzheimer's but are common.
   b. It is often one of the first symptoms in LBD.
3. Motor Symptoms:
   a. Alzheimer's patients usually do not develop significant motor symptoms until the very late stages.
   b. LBD often involves motor symptoms, such as tremors and stiffness, similar to Parkinson's disease, early in the progression.
4. Fluctuations in Cognition:
   a. Cognitive abilities in Alzheimer's generally decline steadily over time.
   b. LBD patients experience pronounced fluctuations, with periods of clarity followed by periods of confusion.
5. Sleep Disorders:
   a. REM sleep behavior disorder is a hallmark of LBD
   b. This is uncommon in Alzheimer's.

6. Response to Medications:
    a. Individuals with LBD are highly sensitive to certain medications, particularly antipsychotics, which can worsen symptoms.
    b. Alzheimer's patients typically do not have the same level of sensitivity.
7. Neurological Basis:
    a. Alzheimer's is associated with the accumulation of beta-amyloid plaques and tau tangles in the brain.
    b. LBD involves the deposition of alpha-synuclein protein, forming Lewy bodies.

Understanding these distinctions is critical for accurate diagnosis and treatment, as misdiagnosis can lead to inappropriate and potentially harmful interventions.

The Impact on Family Members

The effects of LBD extend far beyond the individual diagnosed with the condition. Family members often assume the role of primary caregivers, which comes with significant emotional, physical, and financial challenges.

1. Emotional Strain: Watching a loved one's personality, abilities, and independence decline can be heartbreaking. The unpredictable nature of LBD's symptoms—particularly fluctuating cognition and

hallucinations—can create additional stress and uncertainty.
2. Caregiver Burden: Providing care for someone with LBD often requires round-the-clock attention, especially as the disease progresses. This can lead to caregiver burnout, feelings of isolation, and physical health issues.
3. Financial Impact: The costs associated with LBD can be significant, including medical expenses, home modifications, and the potential need for professional caregiving or long-term care facilities.
4. Family Dynamics: The stress of caregiving can strain relationships among family members, particularly if there are disagreements about care decisions or uneven distributions of responsibilities.

Support and Coping Strategies

Despite the challenges, there are resources and strategies that can help families navigate life with LBD:

- Education: Learning about the disease can empower families to anticipate and manage symptoms more effectively.
- Support Groups: Connecting with others who understand the journey can provide emotional support and practical advice.

- Respite Care: Taking breaks from caregiving responsibilities can help prevent burnout and maintain overall well-being.
- Professional Guidance: Working with neurologists, occupational therapists, and other specialists can ensure a comprehensive approach to care.

Research and Treatment

The field of research on Lewy Body Dementia is growing, with advancements aimed at improving diagnosis, understanding the disease mechanisms, and developing effective treatments. Key areas of focus include:

1. Improved Diagnostic Tools: Researchers are working on biomarker tests, including blood tests, cerebrospinal fluid analysis, and advanced imaging techniques, to detect LBD earlier and more accurately.
2. Understanding Disease Mechanisms: Studies on the role of alpha-synuclein, neuroinflammation, and genetic factors are helping to unravel the complex biology of LBD.
3. Symptomatic Treatments: While there is currently no cure for LBD, various treatments target specific symptoms:

a. Cognitive Symptoms: Medications like cholinesterase inhibitors can help manage cognitive decline and hallucinations.
   b. Motor Symptoms: Dopaminergic drugs may improve motor function, though their use requires careful monitoring.
   c. Behavioral Symptoms: Non-pharmacological approaches, such as therapy and environmental modifications, are often prioritized due to medication sensitivity.
4. Potential Disease-Modifying Therapies: Experimental treatments, including immunotherapies and small molecule drugs targeting alpha-synuclein, are being investigated in clinical trials.
5. Supportive Care Innovations: Advances in assistive technologies and personalized care plans are improving the quality of life for individuals with LBD and their families.

www.ingramcontent.com/pod-product-compliance
Lightning Source LLC
LaVergne TN
LVHW092055060526
838201LV00047B/1404